National Park Explorers

GRAND CANYON

by Sara Gilbert

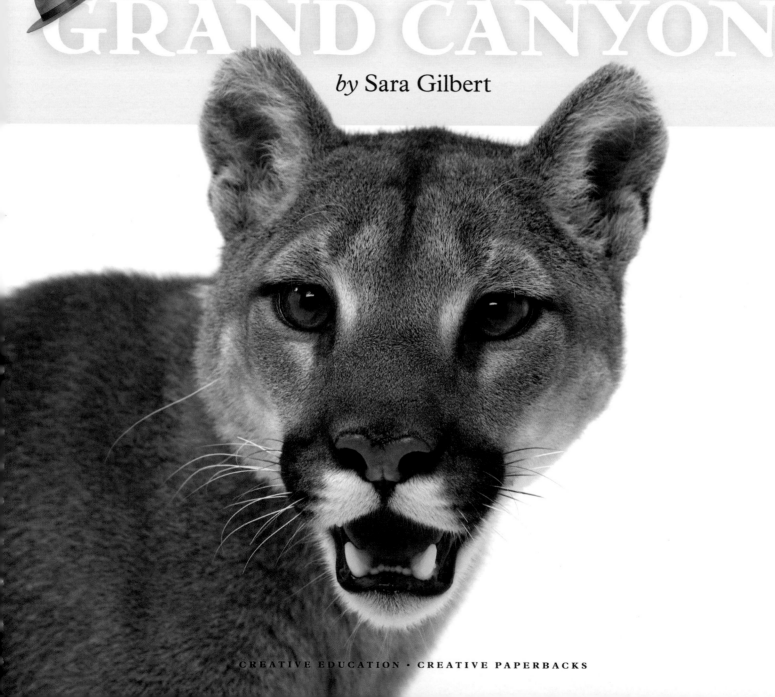

CREATIVE EDUCATION • CREATIVE PAPERBACKS

TABLE OF CONTENTS

Storm clouds gather above the Grand Canyon.

WELCOME TO GRAND CANYON NATIONAL PARK!

Wow! Look at all that rock! At the Grand
Canyon, you can look deep into the earth.
Some of the rocks are millions of years old.

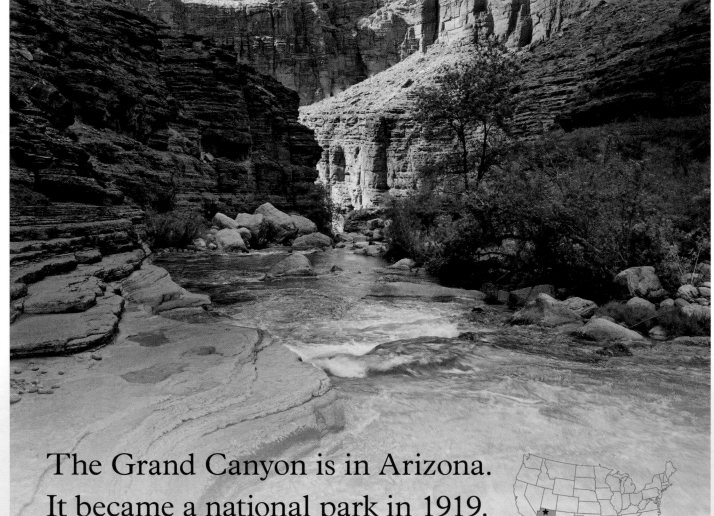

The Grand Canyon is in Arizona. It became a national park in 1919. It is one of the most popular national parks in the United States.

★ Grand Canyon National Park
■ Arizona

Havasu Creek (above); Toroweap Overlook (right)

ROCKS AND A RIVER

The Grand Canyon covers more than one million acres (404,686 ha). Some of it is **desert**. Other parts have lots of trees. It is cooler in the forests.

The Colorado River runs through the Grand Canyon. It made the canyon walls. The rock layers are different colors. People can find **fossils** in the rock.

A fern fossil (below); the Colorado River (right)

CANYON CREATURES

More than 500 kinds of animals and birds live here.
The **endangered** California condor is one of them.
Condors are the biggest birds in North America.

13

There are about 2,000 kinds of plants in the park. A few are found only in the Grand Canyon. They do not grow anywhere else.

14

A cactus (above); a white fir tree (right)

BEAUTIFUL VIEWS

Almost 5 million people visit in a year. You can ride a bus around the rim. You can hike down into the canyon. You can even raft on the Colorado River.

It can get very hot in the canyon. Drink lots of water. Look out for wild animals like mountain lions, too. Do not try to feed them!

A mountain lion (below); riders on a trail (right)

Sunset at the Grand Canyon is a special time. Watch the sun sink below the beautiful rocks!

Park visitors can see across the canyon for miles.

Activity

CANYON CREATION

Materials needed:
Sand box or pile of sand
Hose or bucket of water

Step 1: Create a flat, thick area of sand. This will be the earth.

Step 2: Starting at one end of the sand, pour some water on it to make a river. What happens to the sand as the river runs through it?

Step 3: Add more water. Pour some of it quickly and some of it slowly. How does the speed affect what happens to the sand? Does the path of the river change? What happens to the walls around it?

Glossary

canyon — a deep valley with rocky walls

desert — a hot, dry land that gets little rain

endangered — at risk of dying out, or disappearing from Earth

fossils — the remains of plants or animals found in rocks

rim — the outer edge

Read More

McHugh, Erin. *National Parks: A Kid's Guide to America's Parks, Monuments, and Landmarks*. New York: Black Dog & Leventhal, 2012.

Petersen, David. *Grand Canyon National Park*. Danbury, Conn.: Children's Press, 2001.

Websites

Kids Discover: National Parks
http://www.kidsdiscover.com/spotlight/national-parks-for-kids/
See pictures from the parks and learn more about their history.

WebRangers
http://www.nps.gov/webrangers/
Visit the National Park Service's site for kids to find fun activities.

Note: Every effort has been made to ensure that the websites listed above are suitable for children, that they have educational value, and that they contain no inappropriate material. However, because of the nature of the Internet, it is impossible to guarantee that these sites will remain active indefinitely or that their contents will not be altered.

Index

Published by Creative Education and Creative Paperbacks
P.O. Box 227, Mankato, Minnesota 56002 • Creative Education
and Creative Paperbacks are imprints of The Creative Company
www.thecreativecompany.us

Design and production by Christine Vanderbeek
Art direction by Rita Marshall
Printed in the United States of America

Photographs by Alamy (Rick & Nora Bowers, George H.H. Huey,
Inge Johnsson), Corbis (John Barger, Tom Bean, Neale Clark/Robert
Harding World Imagery, Patrick J. Endres/AlaskaPhotoGraphics,
Frank Krahmer, Joel W. Rogers, Scott Smith, Derek Von Briesen/
National Geographic Creative), Dreamstime (Wisconsinart),
Getty Images (Kick Images), Shutterstock (Tarchyshnik Andrei,
Galyna Andrushko, fivespots, Ronnie Howard, Eric Isselee, Anna
Kucherova, mundoview, ozoptimist, Pacific Northwest Photo, Danny
Smythe, taviphoto, Ultrashock, Rob van Esch)

Library of Congress Cataloging-in-Publication Data
Gilbert, Sara. • Grand Canyon / by Sara Gilbert. • p. cm. —
(National park explorers) • *Summary*: A young explorer's introduc-
tion to Arizona's Grand Canyon National Park, covering its desert
and forest landscape, plants, animals such as California condors, and
activities such as hiking. • Includes index. • ISBN 978-1-60818-632-7
(hardcover) • ISBN 978-1-62832-240-8 (pbk) • ISBN 978-1-56660-
669-1 (eBook) • 1. Grand Canyon National Park (Ariz.)—Juvenile
literature. I. Title.

F788.G466 2016
979.1'32—dc23   2014048723

CCSS: RI.1.1, 2, 3, 4, 5, 6, 7, 10; RI.2.1, 2, 3, 5, 6, 7; RI.3.1, 3, 5, 7;
RF.1.1, 3, 4; RF.2.4

First Edition HC 9 8 7 6 5 4 3 2 1
First Edition PBK 9 8 7 6 5 4 3 2 1